SPORTS RACING LEGENDS

1969 ZINK-VOLKSWAGEN DAYTONA PROTOTYPE

DON RECUPIDO
PHOTOGRAPHY BY JEFF CATT

Acknowledgements:

Dedicated to Breeze, Michael, Jenson and Evan. Thank you for putting up with all my shenanigans throughout the years. I love you all to the Moon!

A special thanks to Bob Houston, Doug Zink and Steve Pieper for fielding so many questions in helping us piece the story of this historic car together so carefully.

ISBN 978-0-578-37275-4

Printed and bound in the United States of America

TABLE OF CONTENTS

PREFACE

In late 1968, a Volkswagen dealer in Virginia commissioned a prototype race car to be built in order to compete in the endurance race at the 1969 24 Hours of Daytona. The impetus for the project was to showcase the fuel efficiency of Volkswagen's new fuel-injected motor launched in the VW Squareback that year. Designated the "Type 3E," the engine in the 1968 VW Squareback was the first use of electronic fuel-injection (EFI) in a German production vehicle and arguably the first "true" modern fuel injected engine. Less fuel meant less time in the pits for refueling, providing a competitive advantage and perhaps some publicity in the process. With early success at Daytona came public factory support and additional funding. The Z-8 became Volkswagen's first racing car and was part of the beginning chapter of the company's involvement with motorsports, which ended in December of 2020 with the launch of the ID.4 electric endurance racer. This is the story of the people who combined a small, efficient motor into a lightweight car to create an endurance racing miracle….

Zink Cars (1962-1974)

Ed Zink owned a small dealership in Knoxville, TN, selling and servicing imported sports cars. Ed's interest in cars started early in life and Ed began his racing career during the early 1950's, driving a dirt-track roadster powered by a Chevrolet six-cylinder engine.[1] Within a few years his interest shifted to road racing and in 1960 Zink designed and built his first road racing car, the Zink Petite MkI. The MkI was a racing car built according to SCCA H-Modified class rules. The car was powered by an 850 cc (52 cu in) DKW engine and mated to a four-speed ZF transmission. The fiberglass body was courtesy of the Jabro MK3. Another car, the MkII was built in 1963.[2] The knowledge and experience gained creating the Petite went into the MKII and the result was a far superior machine. The engine was placed amidships and sent power to the rear wheels.

Right: Zink Cars Circa 1968 *(Figure 1)*

There were only three MkII cars ever created, with two being powered by DKW engines and one by a Coventry-Climax FWA unit. Disc brakes could be found at all four corners and the custom fiberglass body was positioned over an independent suspension. The MkII was enough to prove the manufacturer's potential, when Bill Greer was able to navigate it to an SCCA National Championship in 1963 for the H-Modified class. Bill came to provide much of the funding for Ed's sports cars development with an attempt to create a spec-Volkswagen sports racing class, the Sports Racer Vee (SRV) in the mid-1960's. The Mk designation was dropped for the last two cars and the cars were renamed Z-4. Ed's subsequent racing cars followed the same naming designation. The Tennessee constructor introduced the Zink Z-5 Formula Vee in 1965 and was dominant in its class until 1970. During his career, Ed Zink designed and built over 27 race cars. The Z-8 was his 8th, and his linkage to Volkswagen through Formula Vee proved to be a catalyst for one of his greatest cars.

Upper Left: 1960 Zink Petite MK I (*Figure 2*)

Lower Left: 1964 Zink Z–4 (*Figure 3*)

Hugh Heishman and HRH Corp. (1967-1970)

During the late 1960's through the 1980's, Hugh Heishman was the owner of the Joe Heishman VW dealership in Arlington, Virginia. Heishman inherited the dealership from his father, Joe, earlier in the 1960's, and was one of the first Volkswagen dealers in the United States. Heishman had been actively involved in racing for several years by the late 1960's, after seeing a Mustang perform at a Virginia International Raceway, sparking his interest in racing. Heishman's dealership had been selling Volkswagen Type 3s since its introduction at the 1961 Frankfurt Motor Show. The Type 3 was marketed as the Volkswagen 1500 and later as the Volkswagen 1600, in three body styles: two-door Notchback, Variant and Fastback, the latter being marketed as the "Squareback" in the United States. The Type 3 diversified Volkswagen's product range beyond the existing models – the Type 1 Beetle, the Type 14 Karmann Ghia, and the Type 2 Bus – while retaining several of the Beetle's key engineering principles, notably the air-cooled rear-engine, rear-wheel drive layout and all-round torsion bar suspension on the same 2,400 mm (94.5 in) wheelbase. The concept of the Type 3 was to be more of a family car than the Beetle, offering more passenger and luggage space with a larger engine.

Above: Hugh Heishman in 1969 *(Figure 4)*

The Type 3 followed the Type 1 Beetle but utilized a low-profile version of Volkswagen's 4-cylinder air-cooled engine. In 1968, the Type 3E (Einspritzung) became the first German automobile in series production with electronic fuel injection (EFI) as standard equipment. This configuration ultimately enabled the creation of an unlikely competitor in the endurance racing world.

The Electrojector was available on the 1958 Chrysler 300D, DeSoto Adventurer, Dodge D-500, and Plymouth Fury. This was the first true application of EFI on a production car. The patents for the Electrojector were subsequently sold to Bosch, who developed the Electrojector into the Bosch D-Jetronic. The "D" in D-Jetronic stands for Druckfühlergesteuert, or German for "pressure-sensor controlled."[3] This was a speed/density system, using engine speed and intake manifold air density to calculate "air mass" flow rate and thus fuel requirements, optimizing energy extraction from the fuel. In 1968, the 36-year-old Heishman recognized a significant advantage of the Bosch D-Jetronic system… fuel efficiency. While not normally a factor in short distance (or sprint) racing, fuel efficiency is a major factor in endurance events. Heishman calculated that the stock VW drivetrain, in a lightweight car, could potentially make it competitive with faster cars of the period.

Left: 1969 VW Type 3 *(Figure 5)*

Left: John (Johnny) Moore in the 1968 HRH Chevrolet Camaro *(Figure 6)*

Heishman was an experienced team owner and raced several endurance cars through his HRH racing team at Sebring and Daytona. Heishman presented the idea of using the engine in a sports racing car to his service manager John Moore. John was familiar with Ed Zink's Z-5 Formula Vee and raced them closely in Sports Car Club of America (SCCA) several times. He suggested Zink as a possible manufacturer.

With an idea for the car, Heishman approached Ed Zink in April of 1968 with the concept; incorporate the "Type 3" engine advantages (package size and fuel efficiency) into a sports racing prototype to compete in endurance racing. Discussions about the car followed over the next several months, with Ed borrowing on his success from earlier sports-racer designs. Zink, as a manufacturer was also attractive to Heishman as they helped circumvent the FIA's manufacturing rule by the company having made more than 25 cars total. This rule prevented just anyone from entering the series as it was the "International Championship for Makes."

By Summer of 1968, a design incorporating the improved "Type 3" engine, ball-joint front suspension and transmission was decided on. Ed would develop a frame design to accommodate the newer components, while utilizing part of the "old" Z-4 bodywork. The work was commissioned, and Ed began on the car. Hugh began to envision a grander vision for the project and help in footing the bill.

Formula Vee and Volkswagen

Mercedes' tragedy at the 1955 24 Hours of Le Mans left an indelible mark on German motor racing. The Le Mans incident was a major crash that occurred on the 11th of June 1955 during the 24 Hours of Le Mans motor race at Circuit de la Sarthe in Le Mans, France.[4] Large pieces of debris flew into the crowd, killing 83 spectators, French driver Pierre Levegh, and injuring nearly 180 more. It remains the most catastrophic crash in motorsport history and prompted Mercedes-Benz to retire from motor racing until 1987. Volkswagen adopted an official policy to not support motorsport development through the early 1960's.

Even with Volkswagen's policy, their cars weren't strangers to competition. In response to doubts regarding the Beetle's long-term reliability, Prince Alfonso de Hohenlohe, a friend of Ferdinand Porsche and a car enthusiast resident of Mexico City, decided to enter seven VW sedans in 1954 Carrera Pan Americana competition. All the Beetles finished the 3211 km race.

Right: Type I Beetle "race" cars at the Carrera Pan Americana in 1954 *(Figure 7)*

Left: 1965 Formcar–
Porsche Formula Vee
(Figure 8)

While none finished in first place, the VWs had stock 1200cc engines. Some newspapers reported rumors that the engines were Porsche instead of Volkswagen. An expert mechanic from Houston, Texas, inspected the cars and certified that they had original, unmodified VW engines. The enthusiasm tied to these cars led to the creation of Volkswagen Mexicana, S.A., and Hohenlohe founded the Distribuidora Volkswagen Central, S.A. de C.V. (Central Volkswagen Distributor).[5]

The introduction of Formula Vee in 1962 and subsequent success in the United States and Europe led to some "unofficial" Volkswagen support for the cars. Of course, the "Vee" in Formula Vee clearly meant Volkswagen. This presented the company opportunities for promotion through motorsports, without having to officially change their stance. Porsche purchased five Formcar Formula Vee cars in early 1965 and developed them with the aid of Volkswagen. The first presentation of these "Volkswagens" took place at the Eberbach Hill Climb competition in May 1965. Many well-known racing drivers of the 60's started their career in these single seaters. Just to name a few: Emmerson Fittipaldi, Gijs van Lennep, Ben Pon, Gerhard Mitter, Hans Hermann, etc. In 1966, a promotional tour was set up for the cars, and of utmost importance was the support of Volkswagen CEO Dr. K. Hahn. Over time, the performance of the cars improved, and the series became more important to Volkswagen. Still, funding was hard to come by, and convincing Volkswagen leadership to compete against the likes of Porsche and Ferrari wasn't likely easy.

Z-8 Development

Heishman approached Volkswagen with an idea for the car, and a deal was struck. Volkswagen would provide a "Type 3E" engine, transmission, and front suspension directly off the production line to be used in the car. Terms of the deal included removal of any Volkswagen livery on the car and an unknown amount of direct funding. Heishman was elated, and the new parts were shipped directly to Zink's workshop. Zink was to use a mild steel space-frame chassis under a fiberglass body for the Z-8. Prior versions of his sports-racer designs were not easily adaptable to the new suspension and motor combination. The front suspension of the "Type 3" was a bolt-on subassembly, whereas the earlier cars used a double-wishbone front suspension. This "bolt-on" configuration was not new for Zink, as it was used on his championship winning Formula Vees. The rear suspension also differed from Zink's earlier sports cars but was identical to the setup in the Formula Vee, utilizing stock Volkswagen swing axles and a coil-over shock absorber with a "Z-Bar" to improve traction in tight corners. The "Type 3" axle tubes were deemed too wide for the setup, so the earlier "Type 1" tube was used to get the desired rear track. Zink went to work on the chassis in the Fall of 1968, and the frame was completed in early December of 1968.

Above: Type 3 VW Engine *(Figure 9)*

At this point, the maiden race was only two months away, and much development was still needed to get the car race ready. The existing Z-4 bodywork proved to be about 2 inches too narrow and was widened to accommodate the width of the stock "Type 3" front suspension. As the months progressed, Heishman began to worry that the car might not be ready in time, so he sent several service technicians to Knoxville to help with the work. By early January, the decision was made to transport the car to Heishman's dealership in Virginia to complete the build. The Heishman team worked tirelessly to finish the car through late January 1969, with Hugh Heishman lending a hand as well. Due to time constraints, little work was done to the stock powertrain. The single manifold EFI unit was used from the production car with minor electrical modifications to optimize power at the top of the rev range, where the engine would spend most of its time during the race. BOSCH and Volkswagen of America provided engineering support to help with the modifications during the build.

**Upper and Lower Right:
Assembly at Heishman's
dealership**

(Figures 10 and 11)

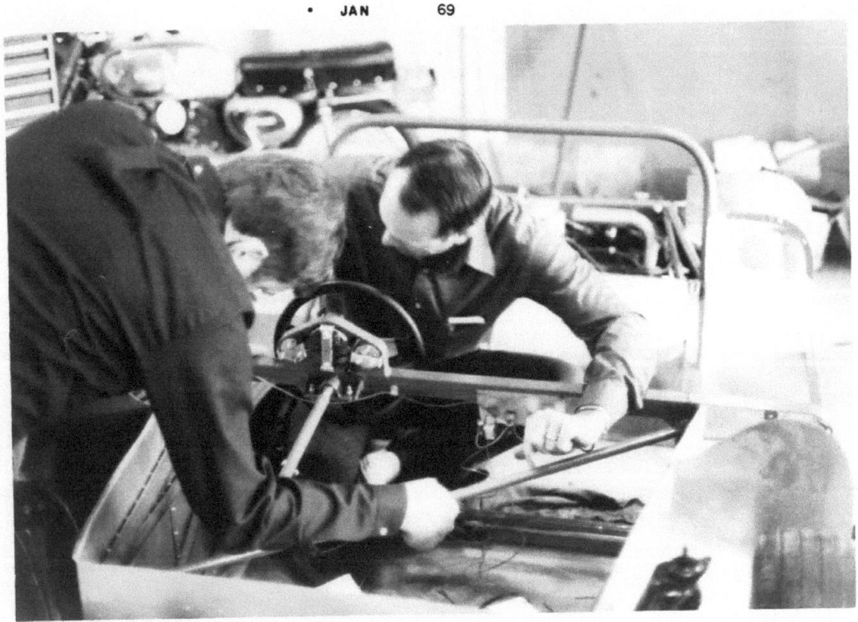

Upper Left: Hugh Heishman working on the Zink Z-8

(Figures 12,13 and 14)

Below: Modifying the fiberglass body

Lower Left: Unfinished Zink Z-8 bodywork

Upper Right: Additional
work on the body

(Figures 15,16 and 17)

Upper: Completed car
in March 1969

Lower Right: Completed
engine installation

1969 24 Hours of Daytona

For the inaugural race of the FIA's 17th season, the car was transported to Daytona, Florida, the week before the race. Work on the car continued until the day before the first of four practice runs on January 29 and 30th. The lighting system had not been completed on the car and was finished at the track. Stock Volkswagen headlights were affixed into the buckets with a metal strap and duct tape. No headlight covers were installed, lending a slightly unfinished look to the car. The body work was modified to accept the Cibie driving lights and Volkswagen Bus license plate lights were added to the sides of the car in order to illuminate the car numbering the night. The car qualified with only a gleaming, white gelcoat and stickers applied for car numbering, along with Heishman's dealership logos. Electrical tape was used create the racing stripes between sessions, and a few supplier "stickers" were added to help the car "go faster". The car was finally ready for the track.

Left: Completed Zink Z–8 at Daytona *(Figure 18)*

The car was driven by three well-known Formula Vee racing drivers: Bill Scott, Steve Pieper, and Jim McDaniel. Pieper and McDaniel were employees of the Heishman dealership, with McDaniel having driven a Porsche 911R for Heishman in both the 1967 Daytona and Sebring events. Bill Scott and Steve Pieper were SCCA Formula Vee drivers, but this was to be the first professional race for both. Pieper was still enrolled at the University of Auburn, pursuing his business degree at the time. Volkswagen provided an RV that afforded the drivers a place to rest during driving breaks, and the CEO of Volkswagen America was in attendance for the race. Several VW technicians were on-hand to help with any technical issues that arose with the new fuel-injection setup.

Qualifying began on February 2nd and the team qualified 52nd overall, but 3rd in the Prototype 2 Liter Class (P2.0). Bear in mind that the slightly modified stock Volkswagen engine only produced 70hp in racing trim and was sharing the track with equipment from Porsche and Ferrari producing over 350hp. The race began at 3:00PM EST, with the tiny Zink sneaking through the last Le Mans-Style start in Daytona history.

Above Left: Bill Scott *(Figure 19)*

Above Right: Jim McDaniel *(Figure 20)*

Steve Pieper (not pictured)

Left: The Z-8 racing through the Daytona infield *(Figure 21)*

Due to the length of the race, Steve Pieper was chosen to take the first stint, as he was the youngest member of the driving crew. With a starting place in the rotation, he would spend the most time in the car during the evening hours, thinking that his youth would give an edge during the night driving period. Over the next 24 hours, vastly more powerful machinery succumbed to the brutal laps, one-after-another. Four of the much faster factory Prototype 3 Liter Class (P3.0) Porsche 908s suffered the same gear failure. The P2.0 class leading Ferrari Dino suffered a head gasket failure on lap 152. The Zink prototype proved to not be immune to mechanical failure, either. Tire issues troubled the team throughout the race and the windscreen flexed so much at top speed, that bracketry was added during the race to stiffen it. A plumbing design issue allowed fuel from the left-side fuel tank to transfer to the right-side fuel tank during the race, due to the forces created on the famous Daytona banking. Fuel stops now included transferring fuel from one tank to the other. The only significant mechanical failure happened during Bill Scott's stint, where the throttle cable broke on the straight before turn 3. The location where he stopped proved to be a godsend, as it was 50 meters from the team's pit area. He rolled to a stop, and the crew ran over to meet him within minutes. FIA's rules were such that mechanics could "help" a driver stranded on the course but could not actually participate in the repair. This could have ended the team's race, but quick-thinking guided Bill to attach a shoestring to the throttle mechanism, operating it by hand to get the car to the pits. Unfortunately, this allowed the #83 Austin-Healy Sprite Prototype to move into 2nd place. At the end of the 24 hours, the Zink managed to hold on to the 3rd spot in class and 18th overall. The jubilant team was rewarded with not only a share of the prize money, but a more serious commitment from Volkswagen, as the corporation took greater interest in the fledgling car.

1969 12 Hours of Sebring

After the Daytona race, the car headed back to the Heishman shop in Virginia. With newfound success came a desire to develop the car further and race at the 12 Hours of Sebring in March of 1969. While placing well at Daytona, the lack of power was evident, and a hurdle for future success. The basic design of the motor and induction system provided an overall limitation on horsepower, and there was room for improvement. The team decided to focus on two main changes for Sebring: engine output and fuel capacity. The engine was pulled from the car for modifications. Two subsequent engines failed during the component testing process. The chassis and bodywork were modified to accommodate twin Daytona-style fuel fillers. The original fuel tank position proved problematic for refueling, as the filler neck was located inside the cockpit. FIA rules allowed for this, but the driver had to exit the car during refueling, creating additional delay during the pitstops. Other minor changes were made, including moving the mirrors from the front fenders to brackets mounted on the windscreen and reshaping the front bodywork slightly to prevent contact with the shock-absorber towers.

Right: Last Le Mans start at Sebring in 1969 *(Figure 22)*

Below: Hugh Heishman with the Z-8 at Sebring *(Figure 23)*

JOE
Heishma
BOSCH

The modifications undertaken would not normally be a difficult challenge for an experienced racing team like Heishman's, as the team had significant experience racing at endurance events; however, this time there were only 48 days from the end of the Daytona race to the first Qualifying session at Sebring, and the car had to make another trip back to Florida. Finally, Volkswagen called to "help."

Racing can be a tricky business. Manufacturer support for a race car that places at the bottom of the field can reflect poorly on the marque. Generally, a privateer effort would not be visibly supported until the car had proven itself over the long-haul. However, this car had a podium at Daytona with a nearly stock engine. What a great promotional opportunity for Volkswagen, right? For the next race, the car was repainted in Porsche Light Ivory with a new Volkswagen livery, adorned with factory badges on the nose and rear deck. "Volkswagen" script was featured prominently on the rear quarter panels. The top of the car was painted in Chevrolet "Lemans Blue," with coves in the front and rear to accommodate car numbering. At Sebring, the team was ready to race without any trackside fabrication. All three drivers completed qualifying laps, with McDaniel setting the qualifying time of 2:32. Gearbox and clutch issues plagued the team during all four qualifying sessions. The car's drivetrain was now tasked with transmitting a lot more power through stickier Goodyear tires. With multiple issues, the Zink qualified 11th out of 13 cars in class and 55th overall. Unfortunately, the Zink would only endure thirteen laps on Saturday's race before clutch issues retired the car. The team returned to Virginia to rethink the season.

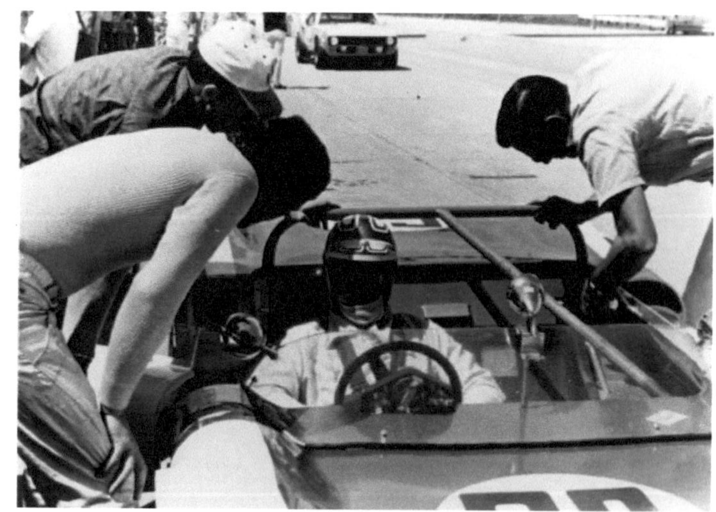

Above: Steve Pieper in the pits for clutch issues *(Figure 25)*

1969 6 Hours of Watkins Glen

Focus for the next race was trained on the gearbox and clutch, which were essentially stock. Stock transmission internals were modified for reliability, and a stouter clutch was sourced from a VW Bus. The hope was that this would fix the issues that forced an early end to the Sebring race. The bodywork was modified with front fender lips (perhaps due to the forecasted rain). The pit crew now included a local Virginia resident named Bob Houston. Bob would bring his significant experience in racing Formula Vees to the Watkins Glen team and would later be part of the car's growing history.

"The Glen" was a storied racetrack, even in 1969. The permanent course was created in 1956 and had hosted Formula One since 1961. Saturday's 6-Hour race was part of a double-feature, with Can-Am cars racing on Sunday. Over 400,000 people attended the race, and the pressure was on to justify the time and money spent on the car. Twenty-nine cars participated in the two Friday qualifying sessions. The Porsche 906E driven by Dick Smothers captured pole position.

Top: Porsche 906E *(Figure 26)*
Middle: Austin Healey Sprite Prototype *(Figure 27)*
Bottom: Unipower GT *(Figure 28)*

The Zink qualified second in class ahead of the two prototype Austin Healey Sprites and the Unipower GT. The race began at 12PM on Saturday July 11, 1969, with cloudy skies. By the end of the first lap, the Zink had lost two positions to faster non-qualifying cars. The immediate start of the race was dry, but a light rain started just a lap later. Harder rain necessitated stops on Laps 12 and 19 to wipe off Pieper's goggles. To the delight of the open-top drivers, the rain stopped, and a dry race line finally appeared. The Zink pitted on Lap 65 for a fuel stop and lost three positions. Soon, several cars fell victim to the rigors of the race, and the Zink moved up to 16th position overall. A fuel and transmission oil stop on Lap 85 didn't change the Zink's fortunes, and it retained its position and finished in 16th place, 2nd in class. A best finish in the car's professional racing career was its last, as Heishman decided to race another car the following year.

Above: Bob Houston (Left) and Ed Zink in 1969 *(Figure 29)*

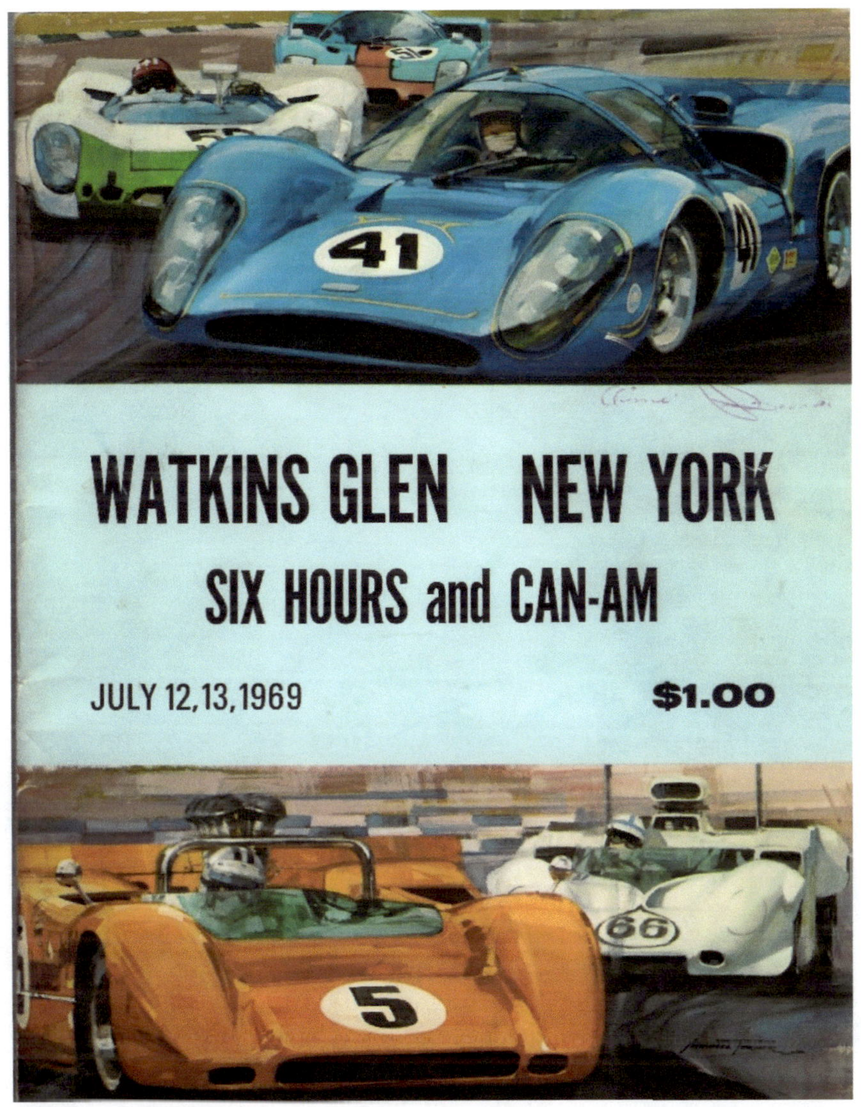

Above: 1969 Watkins Glen race program
(Figure 30)

Right: 1969 Watkins Glen pit pass *(Figure 31)*

Above: Race winning Siffert/Redman Porsche
908/2 *(Figure 33)*

Above: Aerial photo of Watkins Glen prior to
the race *(Figure 34)*

Sports Car Club of America Racing

Bob Houston grew up without interest or a family link to racing. Mostly interested in electronics as a child, Bob had a HAM radio license by the time he was in high school. He clearly had some mechanical aptitude, as he installed a 50ft tall radio tower in the back yard of his parent's house. Bob later upgraded it with a Navy-surplus radar mount that allow him to rotate the 51ft long antenna remotely to get the best reception. By the mid-1960's Bob worked as a technician at an electronics repair company. In 1961, Bob purchased a 1956 Porsche Speedster, but he had a hard time getting local support. With the help of a repair manual, he became his own chief mechanic, and the Speedster became his daily driver for the next 10 years until it became too rusty to drive.

In 1962, a co-worker suggested he join him on a trip to the Formula One Grand Prix at Watkins Glen. The trip ignited Bob's passion for racing, and he returned home with a burgeoning interest in the sport. This inspired Bob to find an unfinished Devin body in the classifieds, then a wrecked VW beetle as a chassis donor. A motor pulled from another Porsche Speedster completed the car, and Bob entered the Devin-Porsche for the first time at Marlboro Raceway in 1964.

Above: Bob racing the Z–8 at the 1970 Summit Point 4–Hour Race *(Figure 35)*

Bob ran the Devin for three seasons, winning the SCCA Regional Championship in 1966. In 1967, Bob picked up a Formcar Formula Vee. Ready for an upgrade in performance the following year, Bob purchased a Zink Z-5 Formula Vee in 1968. By now, Bob was a fixture at Heishman's VW dealer, and had developed a good relationship with the sales manager, Jim McDaniel and Hugh Heishman. Jim invited Bob to crew at Watkins Glen, and Bob jumped at the chance. The race at the Glen was uneventful for the crew, with just a couple of stops. However, it gave Bob a chance to become acquainted with the Z-8. After the race, Heishman offered the car to Bob for $1900 without an engine. Bob purchased the car in October of 1969, with preparations beginning for the 1970 SCCA B-Sports Racing season.

Bob built a new motor for the car right away. For the B-Sports class, it was going to need something with more power. Displacement was left at 1600cc, but upgraded with an EMPI roller crank, 44mm Weber Carburation and an Isky cam. An EMPI 4-into-1 improved exhaust flow and mini-lite wheels finished off the build. Bob's friend owned a used car parts company or "UPAR," and that was soon reflected in the livery for the car.

In early 1970, Bob teamed up with Steve Pieper for a 6-hour race at the newly opened Summit Point. Bob started the race and after 2 hours, the Z-8 was in second place overall. The car was performing well, and Bob stalked the lead Trans-Am Mustang for laps; the Zink was faster just about everywhere on the track except for the long straights. Coming into Turn 10, Bob tried to out-brake the Mustang, locked up the rear and ended up unceremoniously in an infield dirt pile. The car retired early. Parts were bent, but the car was fixed and finished out the rest of the season with a few regional races.

Above: First Place at the 1971 Summit Point 4–Hour Race *(Figure 36)*

Above: In the pits at VIR 1970 *(Figure 38)*

Below: VIR in 1971. Note the roll bar and wheel modifications *(Figure 39)*

Lost to Time and Rebirth

Bob sold the Z-8 to local racer Larry Grim in 1974 to make room for a new Formula Super Vee. Larry raced the car for years and then sold it to local VW aficionado, Bud Williams. Bud stored it without use for at least a decade and at one point loaned it to a friend of his, who later returned the Z-8 describing it as "too much car" for his experience level. At some point the car was disassembled and left outside for several years. Bob knew the whereabouts and condition of the car, but Bud was unwilling to sell it. By 2012, Bob's persistence paid off and Bud accepted Bob's offer to purchase the car back. A trip to the Williams shop was scheduled.

Above Left: Chassis exposed to time *(Figure 40)*

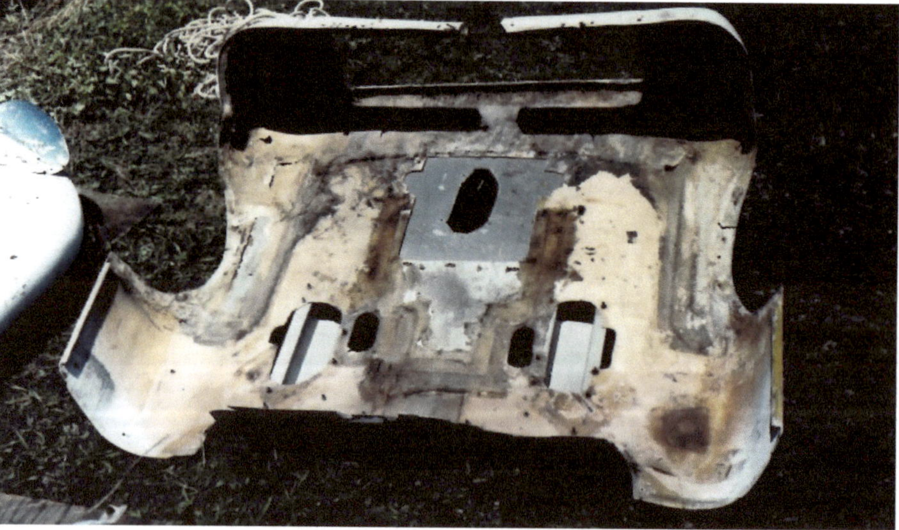

Above Right: The bodywork had numerous modifications *(Figure 41)*

Time and exposure had not been kind to the car. Though the original chassis was still intact, some of the frame tubes needed corrosion repair, and the car needed a complete ground-up rebuild. Having restored many cars in his career, Bob was certainly up for the challenge, and he worked tirelessly on the project for almost five years. Taylor Engineering provided the internals for a new 5-speed gearbox, and Bob built a 1915cc VW engine to power the car, which would still meet the P2.0 historic rules. Reverting to the original drivetrain specs would limit where it could race in vintage events, as most of this racing is short 30-minute sessions not the six, twelve or twenty-four hour races the car was originally designed for. Bob modified the rear bodywork to accommodate a better supported roll bar and larger taillights from a VW bus, both which are significant improvements in safety. Period-correct, fiberglass carburetor covers reminiscent of Jo Sieffert's Porsche 908/2 Flunder were added to protect the powerplant during rainy outings. The original lighting and livery were replicated, with the aesthetics pointing to the 1969 Daytona 24 configuration. In 2017, the car entered its first race in nearly 30 years and has become a regular participant in the vintage racing scene across the United States.

Above Left: Original front bodywork was still intact *(Figure 42)*   **Above Right: On the trailer** *(Figure 43)*

Below and right: Headed home with Bob *(Figures 44 and 45)*

P
JOE
Heishman's
68
GT-1

68
P
Joe
Heishman's

68

JOE
Newman's
P
OFF

WILLANS
WILLANS
OFF
JOE
Heishman's

References

1. www.wikipedia.com, author unknown
   (2021, December 16). *"Zink Cars"*. https://en.wikipedia.org/wiki/Zink_Cars
2. https://zinkpetitemkii.wordpress.com, Hamilton Donaldson
   (2021, November 30). *"Zink Petite MkI and Ed Zink"*. https://zinkpetitemkii.wordpress.com/zink-petite-mk-i-ii-bill-greer/
3. https://en.wikipedia.org/wiki/Fuel_injection, author unknown
   (2021, October 15). *"Fuel Injection"*. https://en.wikipedia.org/wiki/Fuel_injection
4. www.wikipedia.com, author unknown
   (2021, October 16). *"1955 Le Mans Disaster"*. https://en.wikipedia.org/wiki/1955_Le_Mans_disaster
5. https://www.vwvortex.com, *Sebastien@VWvortex*
   (2021, October 16). *"Prince Hohenlohe at the Panamericana: The Race that Made the Beetle a Mexican Star"*.
   https://www.vwvortex.com/threads/prince-hohenlohe-at-the-panamericana-the-race-that-made-the-beetle-a-mexican-star.9451946/

(Figures 1, 4, 10, 11, 12, 13, 14, 15, 16, 17, 18, 19, 20, 21, 23, 24, 29, 35-45) - Original photos provided by Bob Houston

(Figures 2,3) - Hamilton Donaldson

(Figures 5,9) – Volkswagen AG

(Figure 8) - Jan Luehn

(Figures 6, 7, 22, 26, 27, 28, 32-34) - Public Domain

(Figures 30-31) – Don Recupido